MAKE EARRINGS

16 Projects for Creating Beautiful Earrings

QUARRY BOOKS
Rockport, Massachusetts

First published in the United States of America by
Quarry Books, an imprint of Rockport Publishers, Inc.
146 Granite Street
Rockport, Massachusetts 01966-1299
Telephone: (508) 546-9590
Fax: (508) 546-7141

Distributed to the book trade and art trade
in the United States of America by
North Light, an imprint of F & W Publications
1507 Dana Avenue
Cincinnati, Ohio 45207
Telephone: (800) 289-0963

Other Distribution by:
Rockport Publishers, Inc.
Rockport, Massachusetts 01966-1299

ISBN: 1-56496-273-3

10   9   8   7   6   5   4   3   2   1

Designer: Laura Herrmann Design

Printed in Hong Kong
by Regent Publishing Services Limited

CONTENTS

4

EARRING BASICS

14

BEAD IDEAS

18

CREATING A DESIGN

20

Button/Stud EARRINGS

Carnival Beads, 22

Funky Felt Hearts, 26

Pastel Checkerboard Buttons, 30

Tivoli Lights Sunburst Earrings, 34

Colorful Contemporary Earrings, 38

42

Simple Drop EARRINGS

Beaded Hoops, 44

Jeweled Punched Tin Dangles, 48

Wrapped with Style, 52

Gilded Fish, 56

Hoop Dreams, 60

Ivy Leaves, 64

68

Multidrop & Linked EARRINGS

Shades of Blue Earrings, 70

Dazzling Disc Drops, 74

Jewel Bright Triangles, 78

Button People Earrings, 82

Hearts of Gold, 86

Acknowledgments, 90

About the Author, 91

Index, 92

3

EARRING BASICS

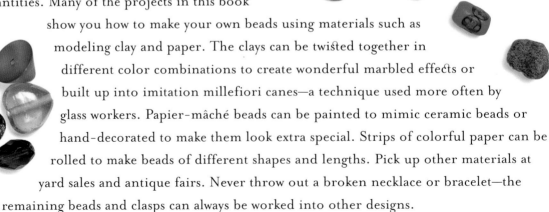

YOU DON'T HAVE TO BE A HIGHLY SKILLED PROFESSIONAL TO CREATE beautiful earrings that make you the envy of your friends. With just a little imagination and the right materials and tools, you can produce wonderful works of art from classic jewelry elements such as beads, precious metals, and stones. Or you can transform mundane, household items such as buttons, fabric scraps, and newspapers into sophisticated earrings. To produce fabulous designs with a professional finish, you will need the findings, tools, and techniques that join, link, and make up your earrings.

Materials

Beads have been used in jewelry making since the beginning of time, but they can be expensive to buy in large quantities. Many of the projects in this book show you how to make your own beads using materials such as modeling clay and paper. The clays can be twisted together in different color combinations to create wonderful marbled effects or built up into imitation millefiori canes—a technique used more often by glass workers. Papier-mâché beads can be painted to mimic ceramic beads or hand-decorated to make them look extra special. Strips of colorful paper can be rolled to make beads of different shapes and lengths. Pick up other materials at yard sales and antique fairs. Never throw out a broken necklace or bracelet—the remaining beads and clasps can always be worked into other designs.

JUMP RINGS are circular or oval metal rings that are not completely joined together. They come in a variety of sizes and thicknesses to suit all kinds of jewelry projects. Use them to link two findings together.

EARRING FITTINGS come in all shapes and sizes, for both pierced and unpierced ears. Hoops, clip earrings, post earrings, and hooks are the most common earring styles. They are also available with ornate designs, or with one or more integral loops or holes to hang more than one drop. The simplest fitting for pierced ears is a hook, which can be obtained in hypoallergenic metals. Ear clip fittings are available with or without perforated backs and attached loops.

Almost all jewelry making requires the use of *findings*, which is the jeweler's term for the basic components that connect the pieces of your earrings and give them a neat finish. Findings help each piece hang correctly. They should be the right size for your earrings; if they are in proportion to the materials that you choose, they will help balance the overall design.

Other Findings

HEAD PINS and EYE PINS are wire pins that come in various lengths to link beads to each other or to an earring finding. A head pin, which has a flat head at one end like a blunt dressmaker's pin, is particularly useful for making charms. Eye pins have a preformed loop at one end and are most often used to link together beads or findings.

Use JEWELER'S WIRE when head and eye pins are not long enough, or when the pins are too thick to pass through tiny beads. It is available in gold and silver in many gauges and can be coiled into decorative spiral charms. The finer the gauge of wire, the easier it is to work with. Choose a wire thickness to suit the beads and the overall design, especially if it is a decorative part of the design.

Other findings to use when making jewelry are ornate SPACERS and HANGERS, which often have two, three, or five preformed holes on one side, and a single loop on the other to join to earring fittings. Large BELL CAPS add a decorative cap to earrings, and are perfect for concealing a collection of tassel knots. Join pendant clasps to jump rings to make a charm hang correctly, or directly clamp on to fabric or seed charms. CALOTTE CRIMPS conceal unsightly knots and, with an attached loop, join to a jump ring, eye pin, or bell cap.

The most important findings are jump rings, head or eye pins, jeweler's wire, and earring fittings. These may all sound rather strange now but by the time you have worked through the projects in this book, they will be much more familiar to you. All findings are readily available in craft stores, from bead suppliers, and even in department stores. You can buy them in precious or nonprecious metals.

Tools & Adhesives

All of the projects in this book are easy to make and require little space for their creation—most can be put together at the kitchen table with only the basic tools. Lay down a craft board to protect the table from damage, and provide a flat, even surface to work on. Organize your beads and findings in boxes and trays.

Small round-nosed and needle-nosed pliers, available at jewelry and bead suppliers, make opening, closing, and linking together findings much easier. Use round-nosed pliers to turn loops, and to twist and coil wire into shape. Squeeze calotte crimps together and flatten joints with needle-nosed pliers.

Use two pairs of pliers to open and close jump rings. Buy them with integral wire cutters or invest in a separate pair of wire cutters for trimming head and eye pins, and jeweler's wire.

As a general rule, an all-purpose, clear-drying glue and a stronger, bonding epoxy glue are all you will need to ensure that your wonderful design won't break when you wear it. Take the time to read and follow the directions on the glue container. Use common sense: make sure that bead and finding surfaces are clean and grease-free; and, with some glues, you may need to work in a well-ventilated room.

Linking Beads

Link together groups of beads, in similar or bright, contrasting colors, with head or eye pins to make stunning earrings. You can wire each bead individually, which is quite time-consuming but produces an expensive-looking finish, or work the beads in small groups. To make the beads go further and use up leftover beads, insert short lengths of chain between each group of beads.

To make drops, use a head pin, a particularly useful finding for making drops because the flat head prevents beads from sliding off the pin. If the head pin slips through the bead hole, add a small stopper bead first. Slide the beads onto the pin in the order you want, trim the wire with wire cutters if necessary, and then turn a loop with round-nosed pliers. The loop can then be attached to an earring finding or a jump ring.

Eye pins are ideal for linking beads together because they already have a preformed loop

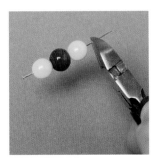

Trimming a head pin already threaded with beads

in one end. Use short pins for single beads and longer ones for groups of beads. Slide the beads onto each pin, trim the wire, and turn a loop, just as you would with a head pin. To link the beads together, use jump rings or open up a loop on the pin and join to the next loop. Make

sure you close the loops securely or they will come undone when you wear them.

You can substitute jeweler's wire for the head and eye pins. To make drops, you will need to turn a small spiral in the end with round-nosed

Turning a loop on the head pin.

pliers. You can then leave this protruding as a decorative effect or turn it under so the bottom bead sits on it. For linking beads, simply turn a loop in each end with pliers.

Multidrop Earrings

To create more elaborate earrings, whether they are clip or post fittings, work with multiple strands or add special tops and other decorative findings.

Multidrop earrings can simply be several bead strands joined to one another or to an end spacer. To make basic multidrop earrings, bead several strands of similar lengths, link the loops of these together in a jump ring, and join the jump ring to an eye pin. Insert the eye pin through the hole of a decorative or filigree bell cap. For an easy variation on this basic design, try alternating the lengths of the drops to create a tasseled effect. Use multidrop hangers that are specifically made for earrings, or attach end hangers that are used

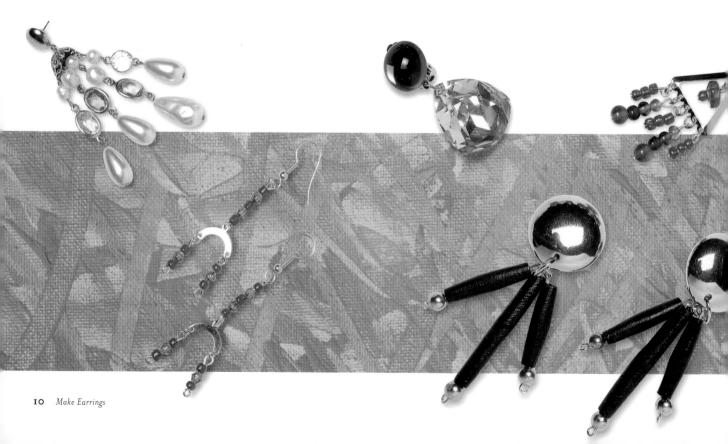

for making necklaces and bracelets. Such hangers can be plain and simple or, if you want to make more decorative pieces, choose hangers encrusted with jewel stones or diamanté. To use hangers, select one with the same number of holes as the number of drops you are using—usually two, three, or five holes. Wire the beads with head or eye pins,

and link them to the finding with jump rings.

Take advantage of the preformed holes in decorative clasps designed for necklaces and bracelets. Glue pierced or clip-on fittings to the reverse side of the clasp and hang beads or bead strands from the clasp holes.

Finishing Techniques

How you finish a pair of earrings can make or break your design. To get a truly professional look, use findings—the tiny metal components used to link, join, and complete a design. Jump rings link together two or more pieces, such as an earring drop to an ear fitting, or several earring drops to one another. To keep the shape of the ring, and to ensure that the two ends

Hold a jump ring with two pairs of pliers positioned at either side of the joint. Gently twist the ends away from each other sideways to open, and twist back again to close.

meet perfectly again, open the rings at the joint using pliers (two pairs of pliers are ideal), twisting the ends away from each other sideways rather than just pulling them apart. To close, simply twist the ends back again so that they meet exactly. Practice opening and closing them successfully.

Although many earrings are wired with head or eye pins, beaded threads are sometimes used to allow the earring drop to hang more fluidly. End knots on such threads can look ugly and need to be disguised. For most earrings, a calotte crimp is

Place the knot at the end of a length of thread in the cup of a calotte crimp and squeeze the two halves together using needle-nosed pliers.

usually sufficient; its preformed loop can be joined to a jump ring and earring fitting, or to an eye pin and bell cap.

There are several calotte crimp designs to choose from. Round calottes look like tiny metal beads when they are closed. They are hinged either at the side or bottom and have a gap for the thread to pass through. For sideways-opening calottes, position the knot in the "cup" of one half and use needle-nosed pliers to squeeze the two sides together. Make sure the thread is going in the right direction before you secure the crimp. If you are using calottes that open from the loop end, you will need to pass the thread through a small gap in the hinged end before knotting, then close in the same way as before. Use square calottes for thick cord or thong; they are open on one side, which is where you insert the thread. With needle-nosed pliers, fold one side over the thread and then the other side to secure the thread. An alternative is crimp beads, tiny metal beads, that hold loops in the ends of nylon line or tiger tail. Simply thread them into position and squeeze firmly with pliers to secure.

Use calottes on multidrop earrings when you are attaching a decorative end spacer, or if the design has lots of strands, add a bell cap to hide the calottes. This is a bell-shaped, metal cap with a central hole. Slip the loops of the calottes onto a jump ring, but before closing the ring, push it through the loop of an eye pin. Insert the pin through the hole in the cap, trim it to about ⅜ inch / 1 cm with wire cutters and turn a loop with

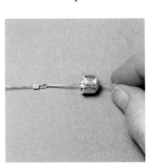

A bell cap conceals a collection of knots or just adds a decorative end to a pair of earrings. Slip the open eye of an eye pin through a calotte loop in the tiger tail. Close it securely. Push the pin through the central hole in the cap, and trim and turn a loop in the opposite end.

round-nosed pliers. Bell caps are often very ornate and come in a variety of sizes. Use the smaller ones as decorative ends on delicate single-strand earrings.

Add metal spacers, findings that are usually associated with necklaces and bracelets, to give decorative detail and polish to drop earrings. Spacers are available in a range of sizes and styles, from the highly ornate to the very simple; use a style that matches the scale and complexity of your earring design. Spacers work well as the top element of a drop earring or as a link between single beads or a group of beads.

Use metal spacers to add interesting detail to simple drop earrings. The size and style of the metal spacer suits the clean, simple lines of these beaded drops.

BEAD IDEAS

A VISIT TO YOUR LOCAL CRAFTS STORE WILL REVEAL AN array of beads to use in making your earrings. Or be adventurous and use objects you can find at home, such as pasta shapes or feathers from a feather duster, to substitute for beads. If you choose to make your own beads, try unusual materials, such as newspaper and magazine cuttings, colored foil, or fabric scraps.

Clay Beads

One of the most effective materials to use is polymer clay. It is available in a fantastic range of colors, molds easily, and sets hard in a low-temperature oven. There are several comparable brands available, each with their own malleability, baking time, and color selection.

Plain beads in a single color can be molded into any shape you want and then decorated with acrylic paints (water-based paints don't cover as well). To make the beads, first knead the clay until it is soft and pliable, then roll it out into a log shape, ¼ to ¾ inch / .5 to 2 cm in diameter, depending on how big you want the bead to be. For tube beads, cut the log into equal lengths and pierce the center with a toothpick or knitting needle. Pierce the bead from both ends to get neat holes; if you just push the stick straight through, make sure that you smooth the rough edges where the stick emerges.

Round beads are made in the same way but each piece of clay is shaped into a ball in the palms of your hands. Pierce holes with a toothpick as above. Square beads are also made from a long log that is then flattened into a square against the edge of a knife or piece of wood. Cut to size and pierce as before. Add texture and detail to plain beads of any shape by pressing modeling tools, coins, and so on, against the surface, or by adding small strips or dots of other colors.

Experiment with several colors, for more exciting finishes, such as marbling or millefiori. To create a marbled effect, roll out logs of two or more colors and wrap them around each other. Knead these together, roll them back into a larger log, folding it in half and twisting until the colors are blended. Be careful not to knead too much or the individual colors will disappear and the clay will eventually return to a new, single color. Shape beads as described above.

Millefiori or "thousand flower" beads, are slightly more complicated, but rewarding to make once you have mastered the techniques. Begin with a core color—either a plain log or two colors rolled together. Then place other logs in different colors around the core, completely surrounding it. The colors are usually placed in a regular pattern and must be gently pressed together to ensure no air is trapped inside. The whole cane is then wrapped in another sheet of clay, carefully rolled out to a diameter of about ¼ inch / .5 cm, and cut into tiny slices that are pressed on an unbaked base bead to cover it.

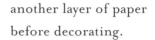

Paper Beads

Using paper is one of the easiest and cheapest ways to make beads. The simplest papier-mâché beads can be made by shaping pieces of newspaper into a ball and then layering pasted strips of newspaper over it. For a smoother finish, layer the paper strips over a ball of plasticine. When the ball is completely dry, cut it in half with a craft knife and remove the plasticine to lighten the paper beads. Glue the two halves of the bead back together and conceal the joint with another layer of paper before decorating.

To make rolled paper beads, use old wrapping paper or magazines, or paint your own designs onto plain paper; then cut into strips or elongated triangles, and roll up tightly around a toothpick. To give the finished beads a sheen and a durable finish, paint them with clear nail polish.

Fabric Beads

You can use fabric to make all kinds of beads that can be decorated with embroidery or sewn stitches, or even with tiny beads. To make little puffs of fabric, cut the fabric out in circles, hem the edges, and draw up the edges. For tube beads, strips of fabric can be joined and gathered at either end. To give them shape, wrap them over a cardboard base or stuff with a little padding.

Wooden Beads & Pressed Cotton Beads

Most craft suppliers stock unvarnished wooden beads and pressed cotton balls in a variety of sizes. These are both easy to paint and decorate in you own individual style.
Support the beads on wooden skewers, tops of pencils, or old paintbrush handles while painting, and leave to dry on a knitting needle stuck in a block of plasticine or polystyrene. Keep patterns simple. If you want to use several colors, let each color dry before starting the next. When you are finished, protect the surface with a coat of clear varnish or nail polish.

Miscellaneous Bead Ideas

Roll ordinary kitchen foil or colored candy foil wrappers to make bead shapes. Pierce the center with a sharp needle and thread into simple drop earrings. Or add colored foil as a decorative final layer on a papier-mâché bead. Salt dough, which needs to bake in a low-temperature oven for several hours, is another good medium for making beads of different shapes. Both foil and clay can be painted and decorated to suit your design.

Pasta, seeds, nuts, and even washers can be painted, decorated, and strung into spectacular earrings—no one will ever guess their origins. Use your imagination, and you will discover that all sorts of bits and pieces—safety pins, colorful paper clips, and even rubber bands can be turned into jewelry.

CREATING A DESIGN

Finding Inspiration

THE STARTING POINT IN ANY DESIGN IS FINDING INSPIRATION.
Ideas for jewelry designs can come from a visit to a museum or a library.
Look to the ancient Egyptian, Roman, and Celtic civilizations, as well as the more recent Arts and Crafts and Art Deco periods, for ideas. A walk in the country or along the seashore can put you in touch with one of the greatest and most economical design source libraries: Mother Nature. Flowers and foliage, rocks and minerals, insect and animal life all can spur the imagination. The sky provides us with the sun, moon, and star motifs that are perfect for interpreting into jewelry forms. The sea washes up shells on the beach and sculpts pebbles and wood into interesting shapes.

Don't forget the materials you have on hand. Beads and fabrics can fall accidentally and often haphazardly together to create striking and unusual combinations. Paints and decorative finishes are fun to experiment with.

Clays can be molded into unusual shapes and given textured finishes.

Working Out a Design

Once you have found your inspiration, try to sketch out different ideas on paper. You will need a sketch book, tracing paper, pencils, colored crayons, felt tip markers (including gold and silver markers), an eraser, and a pencil sharpener. You don't have to draw works of art; rough sketches will suffice. Consider buying a special bead tray with channels for the beads to help you plan your earring designs.

For simple bead earrings, decide on the length you want. Choose between long, dramatic drops, or shorter, more discreet, designs. After working out your basic design, decide on the style of earring fitting you want to use, and whether you will string beads on thread, or wire them on jeweler's wire or head or eye pins. When you calculate how many beads you will need, make sure you have enough for a matching pair of earrings.

Write down the findings you will need next to your design sketch. If you want to try any unusual paint effects or create complex millefiori beads, experiment with paints on paper before moving on to a sample bead.

Bold shape painted with bright enamels

Papier Maché

reverse shape for second earring

Clay heart with tiny heart dangles

Citrus earrings use sharp green, yellow + orange beads

Windchime earrings
Gold + silver bugle beads or mixed glass rocaille

Button/Stud
EARRINGS

E arrings are one of the easiest types of jewelry to produce, and one of the simplest earring styles to make is basic button or stud shapes. Just visit your local jewelry, bead, and craft suppliers to find post, clip-on, or perforated fittings to which you can attach flat-backed cabochon stones or small faceted beads in jewel-bright colors. Slices cut from a wine bottle cork can be painted and beaded to make pretty earrings that bear no resemblance to their humble origins.

Consider the size of the earring design relative to your frame, hairstyle, and face shape—oversized earrings on a petite individual with a chic, gamine haircut look out of proportion and are better suited to taller people with bigger hairstyles. It is also important to position the earring back in the right place, whether it is close to the top of the earrings or with the post or clip dead center. If you have any doubts, use Blu Tak or plasticine to temporarily fix the finding and check in the mirror to see which position looks best. With abstract shapes, make sure the earrings face the same direction on each ear (in mirror images of each other) before permanently fixing the finding in place.

It's easy to reinterpret any of the designs that follow. Cork slices can be painted in any color and decorated with beaded pins, metal spirals, or ornate hand-painted designs. Fabric paints and pens come in such a wide range of colors that they are perfect for experimenting with different pattern ideas, from defined geometric designs to free-flowing, unstructured variations. Abstract papier-mâché shapes provide a great base for intricate hand-painted designs, but they look just as good in plain colors with glamorous jewel stones adding a touch of sparkle.

Carnival
BEADS

Design Tips

Decorate the cork center with a more intricate painted design and bead the pins with coordinating colors.

Ⓢ

To create a spider-web effect, weave colored embroidery threads or jewelry wire in and out of the pins.

Ⓢ

For a totally natural look leave the cork unpainted. Just smooth the surface with an emery board and, making sure it is dust-free, add several coats of varnish to bring out the grain.

Ⓢ

Decorate pins with wooden beads to complement the natural look of the cork.

Ⓢ

Once you have mastered the art of making metal spirals, try winding them out from a small bead center.

Ⓢ

Instead of gluing one striking central bead to the cork, try adding lots of tiny stones at random for a jewel-encrusted finish; then add coordinating bead pins.

MAKING SOMETHING FROM NOTHING IS A REALLY rewarding hobby and once you get started, you'll find potential in the most unusual objects and delight friends with your creativity. It is surprisingly easy disguising the origins of everyday materials to produce stylish pieces of jewelry. These imaginative earrings are made from slices cut off an ordinary wine bottle cork that are then cleverly transformed with a coat of metallic paint and bead decoration. Cork is a particularly versatile material to work with; you can easily paint it and insert beads on pins into it. The ideas illustrated require no special skills or equipment and can be made in a very short time. Use the designs for inspiration to create your own unique interpretations.

Getting Started

Sterilize the cork before you start the project using household bleach or a sterilizing solution from your local pharmacy. Make sure you use clear-drying glue that is suitable for all surfaces.

A cork
Sterilizing solution or bleach
Cutting mat
Craft knife
Emery board
Gesso
Paintbrush
Gold metallic paint
Darning needle or large tapestry needle
Varnish (optional)
14 head pins
A selection of beads
Wire cutters
Clear-drying hobby adhesive
Epoxy or similar strong adhesive
2 flat-backed jewel stones
2 ear clip findings
(or studs if preferred)

CARNIVAL BEADS

When the sterilized cork is completely dry, cut 2 slices approximately ¼ inch / .5 cm thick using a heavy-duty craft knife.

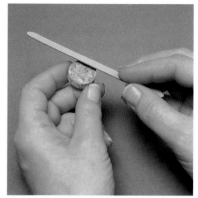

Smooth the surface with an emery board. Brush off any dust residue.

Paint all surfaces with a gesso undercoat. Let dry and then add a coat of gold metallic paint.

Use a thick needle to pierce 7 holes at regular intervals around the edge of the slice. Varnish at this stage if required.

Bead each head pin and trim with wire cutters leaving a length of free wire to insert into holes. Add a tiny blob of clear-drying glue to hold the pins in place.

Variations on a Theme

SILVER SPIRALS

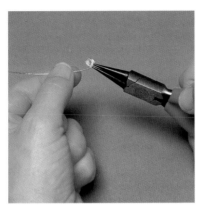

6.

Glue central stones and earring backs in place with the stronger adhesive.

2.

Make holes in the side edge of a painted cork slice as in step 4 above. Insert the spirals, the tips marked with a blob of glue to secure.

1.

Metal spirals are easy to make and give the cork slices a completely different look. Cut a length of jeweler's wire and, with the tip of the pliers, start the spiral by turning a small loop at the end. Wind the wire around the loop until the spiral is the size you want.

3.

Finish with either a clip-on or stud earring back.

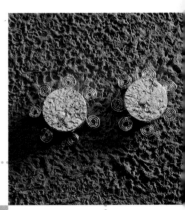

For this variation the cork has been painted black and 8 pins beaded with a single black bead. This idea would also look good with a black center and white beads, or vice versa (right).

Funky Felt
HEARTS

Design Tips

Experiment with different base shapes and color combinations.

◎

Use firm iron-on interfacing to give the finished piece more body if preferred.

◎

Add more intricate embroidery stitches and bead decoration to produce a more sophisticated design.

◎

Experiment with three-dimensional designs such as flowers and insects.

◎

Take the idea of soft jewelry further and embroider and bead canvas shapes as well.

◎

Instant earrings can be made from store-bought motifs cut to size and decorated with more stitches and ornate metal spirals.

◎

Look for design ideas in embroidery books.

THE DISCOVERY OF FELT IS A FASCINATING STORY. According to legend, St. Clement, the patron saint of felt makers, put wool in his shoes to warm his feet and found that the pressure of his feet combined with heat and moisture created a new fabric, felt. This process is essentially how felt is produced, but the fabric existed well before the time of St. Clement, and is probably one of the oldest known to civilization. For the crafter, felt is wonderfully versatile, inexpensive, and available in a stunning array of colors. It is easy to mark and cut, doesn't fray, and can be embellished with any number of decorative effects from embroidery stitches to beads and sequins. For these pretty earrings, felt hearts of decreasing size are glued on top of one another and decorated with the most basic embroidery stitches. These stitches create a naive style, but it is easy to make the earrings look more glamorous by adding more intricate stitchwork.

You Will Need

1 red and 1 green felt square
Pencil
Scissors
Craft glue
Needle
Silk embroidery thread
2 earring backs
(clip-on or post fittings)

Getting Started

Choose silk embroidery to accent the felt colors; look for either matching or contrasting colors. To obtain identical hearts, draw your heart shape on the felt, layer that piece over another, and, following your outline, cut through the two layers of felt.

FUNKY FELT HEARTS

1. Draw your motifs onto the felt in pencil and cut out carefully. You will need 4 large red hearts, 2 green hearts cut slightly smaller, and 2 more red hearts, smaller still. Drawing the motifs onto the felt freehand contributes to a simple look.

2. Glue a green heart in the center, on top of one of the large red hearts. Let dry. Glue the tiny red hearts in place on top of the green hearts in the same way. Let dry.

3. Using 2 or 3 strands of embroidery thread, work a blanket stitch around the outside edge of the earring.

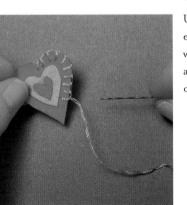

4. Work a tiny running stitch just inside the outside edge of the green heart.

5.

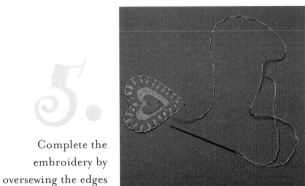

Complete the embroidery by oversewing the edges of the smallest heart.

6.

Trim the edges of the remaining large hearts to make them slightly smaller than the main shape. Glue in place on the reverse side to conceal any knots or ugly stitching. Let dry.

7.

Glue an earring back in place to complete the earrings.

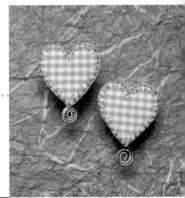

Variations on a Theme

Embroidered and beaded canvas squares are mounted on cardboard to make these earrings (right).

A simple iron-on motif bought from a sewing shop looks wonderful turned into simple earrings. The metal spiral is made from jeweler's wire worked into shape with pliers and is glued in place between the motif and its cardboard backing (far right).

Pastel Checkerboard
BUTTONS

Design Tips

Sketch out your design on paper first and fill in colors with crayons or paints that match your fabric paints.

⊙

Experiment with different textile techniques like tie-dye or batik to create more interesting finishes.

⊙

Back a piece of silky fabric with iron-on interfacing to lend it more substance and to make it easier to fashion into different earring shapes.

⊙

Mount the finished design on cardboard or use self-cover buttons.

⊙

Experiment with the many textured fabric paints available to create different effects.

F ABRIC PAINTING IS A WONDERFUL way to decorate all kinds of textiles and allows you to be totally creative and experimental. The project shown here is simple to work and is designed to inspire you to create your own patterns. The simple geometric design is worked out on paper first and then used as a template. Fabric-painting pens add the color; these are just like felt-tipped pens and give you greater control over where they are placed. To prevent the colors from bleeding into one another, use a special outline resist called gutta, which is also used to outline the design before the color is added. You can buy gutta in lots of different colors including clear, which can be washed out. Fabric paints come in pots just like ordinary paints and are applied with a brush. The colors, which can be fixed with a warm iron, are completely washable.

Getting Started

Cut the silky fabric into a square. (If you want paler finishes, use a synthetic fabric.) Choose a color of gutta that complements the color of the fabric pens you will use. A pearlized gutta was used in this project to highlight the pretty pastel shades.

You Will Need

Cardboard
2 self-cover buttons
Pencil
Ruler
Tracing paper
Silky fabric
Embroidery hoop
Adhesive tape
Gutta and fabric painting pens
Iron-on interfacing
Compass
Scissors
Needle
Thread
2 earring backs
(clip-on or post fittings)
All-purpose craft glue

PASTEL CHECKERBOARD BUTTONS

1.

Place the button base on cardboard and draw around its circumference to get the area of the finished design.

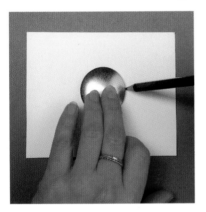

2.

Draw the outline of the pattern or motif on the cardboard and transfer to tracing paper.

3.

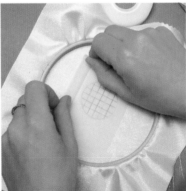

Fix the fabric in an embroidery hoop and tape the motif to the wrong side. Make sure the fabric is taut.

4.

Test the gutta on a fabric scrap to get the feel of the paint flow, then outline the pattern or motif and let dry. Fill in the colors, being careful not to mark the gutta. Do a test piece before starting on the real thing.

5.

Remove the painted design from the hoop and trim the fabric, leaving at least 1 inch / 2.5 cm all around. Iron the interfacing to the wrong side (to fix the colors) and draw a larger circle to the size indicated on the button cardboard.

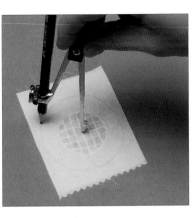

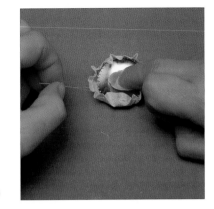

6.

Use pliers to remove the button shank. Then run a gathering thread close to the edge of the outer circle. Place the button in the center of your design and draw up the thread, easing the fabric over the serrated edge.

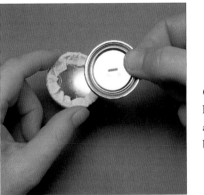

7.

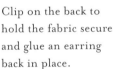

Clip on the back to hold the fabric secure and glue an earring back in place.

Variations on a Theme

This design was achieved by painting the fabric. The first coat was applied with a water-laden brush. Then pink and gold highlights were applied using a fairly dry brush. Let each coat dry before applying the next (right).

Textured paint in a vividly contrasting color was used to add polka-dots to the same painted base used for the previous variation (far right).

Divide your selected beads into two groups—one for each earring—to make sure you have a similar mix of sizes and that the overall color balance is consistent.

❂

You can choose stopper beads to match each bead used or a single neutral color for all points.

❂

Try varying the length of the tassels or attach beaded loops with a large central bead.

❂

Variations on the theme can be worked with beads of the same color and size or same color and varied sizes.

❂

Experiment with different patterns by working in rows from the center point.

Tivoli Lights Sunburst
EARRINGS

THE FABULOUS VARIETY OF BEADS AVAILABLE
in myriad colors is inspiration on its own; it is almost
impossible to choose just a small selection. A
jar of faceted glass beads in a mix of sizes and a kaleidoscopic
range of colors is the inspiration for these ornately beaded
earrings. They are much simpler to make than they look and use
a clever perforated back that allows you to sew thread in and out.
This is then clipped to an earring back to complete the design.
The tassels are a dramatic touch but the basic style of these
earrings has been around for centuries. When working with
such an eclectic mix of colors, it doesn't matter if
each earring in the pair is slightly different as long as
the overall balance of color is the same. Points of
interest, like the tassels, however, are likely to draw
more attention and it is best if these are identical on each.

Getting Started

Allocate 30 to 35 small, faceted beads and 30 to 35 stopper beads for each
earring. The stopper beads, when threaded with the larger beads, secure
the larger bead onto the earring fitting. Cut a length of thread approximately 30 inches / 76 cm long. (You may prefer to work on shorter
lengths and oversew to tie off each end before starting on the next.)

You Will Need

60 to 70 small faceted beads
6 larger beads for tassel ends
60 to 70 stopper beads
Invisible thread or fine nylon line
Beading needle
2 perforated earring
fittings with backs
Glue
Pliers

TIVOLI LIGHTS SUNBURST EARRINGS

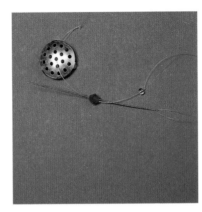

1. Make a large knot in the end of the thread. Take it through the center hole of the perforated fitting from the concave side and add the first bead and stopper bead.

2. Take the needle around the stopper bead and back through the first bead.

3. Bring the needle back through the center hole and through the center of the knot to secure.

4. Bring the needle back to the right side through a hole adjacent to the center point. Add a bead and stopper bead as before and take the needle back to the wrong side. Working in circles following the pierced holes on the perforated fitting, continue in the same way until you have completed the outside edge. Depending on the size of your beads, it may not be necessary to bead every hole—you will have to judge this as you go. Oversew the end of the last thread, working the stitches in and out of the holes on the perforated fitting.

Position the tassels between 2 claws on the perforated fitting to allow enough room to clamp the claws over the earring back. Make a large knot in a piece of thread 12 inches / 30.5 cm long. Thread the needle through the back from the wrong side and add enough beads to make the first tassel. End with a larger bead and stopper bead. Take the thread back through all but the stopper bead and secure on the wrong side. Work the other tassels on both sides in the same way.

Add a dab of glue to all knots and loose ends as a precaution.

Clamp the claws of the perforated fitting over the earring back using pliers.

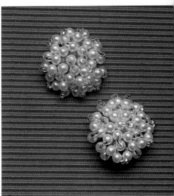

Variations on a Theme

The same techniques are used to create monochromatic earrings from faceted glass beads (right).

Try beading pearls and crystals onto a perforated fitting to create an elegant pair of earrings (far right).

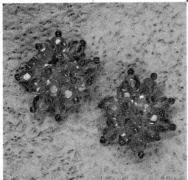

Colorful Contemporary
EARRINGS

Perfect
Papier-Mâché

For perfect papier-mâché,
use torn strips of newspaper:
The rough edges produce less
obvious joints.

Carefully overlap each piece and
smooth the edges with your
fingers to release any trapped
air or lumpy paste.

Use two different colored newspapers
to make it easier to distinguish
between the layers.

You can use wallpaper paste or PVA
glue as an adhesive. Wallpaper paste
is easier to work with because it's less
tacky than PVA, but PVA produces a
stronger finish. Mix the two together
(to a consistency of thick cream), or
use PVA for the last few layers.

All the layers can be applied at once,
but to achieve the smoothest finish,
allow each layer to dry before
applying the next.

Thin cardboard may begin to warp
with the dampness of the paste. To
rectify this, dry it between two baking
sheets with something heavy on top.

THE CRAFT OF PAPIER-MÂCHÉ IS ENJOYING A GREAT revival. It is versatile, inexpensive, and it only needs a small work space, which makes it a great medium for lots of projects, especially in jewelry making. The name means "mashed paper" in French, though it is a term they have only recently recognized. In the nineteenth century it was used to make tables and chairs, which appear from time to time in sales rooms today looking almost as good as new. These striking earrings are made using one of the easiest papier-mâché techniques—layering pasted strips of torn paper over a base shape or mold. It is a very simple process to master and needs only a little care when building up the layers to ensure they are smooth with no air or lumps of paste (unless you want a textured finish).

You Will Need

Firm cardboard
Pencil
Scissors
Wallpaper paste
Paste brush
Small strips of torn newspaper
PVA glue
Emery board
Gesso
Paintbrush
Acrylic artist's paints with
an enamel finish
Fine paintbrush
Gold metallic marker pen
2 earring backs
(clip-on or post fittings)
All-purpose glue
Varnish

Getting Started

This simple papier-mâché project involves pasting small strips of newspaper over a cardboard shape that is then painted with gesso and acrylic artist's paint. Follow instructions on the packet to make a small amount of wallpaper paste.

COLORFUL CONTEMPORARY EARRINGS

1.

Draw 2 identical shapes onto a piece of thick cardboard.

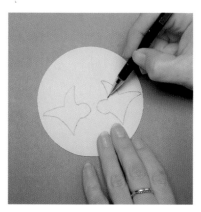

2.

Cut out the shapes carefully, using sharp scissors to get into all the angles.

3.

Paste a strip of newspaper and place on one side of the shape so that a little extends beyond the edge. Smooth flat with your fingers. Smooth the protruding end over to the opposite side, being careful to get it crisp on the edge.

4.

Continue layering pasted strips over the shape, covering both sides and the edges. You will need 4 to 6 layers in all to create a firm, finished piece. Paint the last few layers with PVA glue instead of paste for a durable finish.

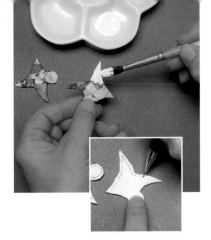

Paint the earrings with artist's gesso. This acts as an undercoat and prevents the newsprint showing through the painted finish. Draw a narrow border around each shape and mark the stripes in faint pencil.

Paint the border with a fine paintbrush. Let dry before painting the pattern in the colors of your choice. You only need to do this on one side of the earring. The wrong side can be painted with the border color. Let each color dry before applying the next.

Outline the design carefully with a gold metallic marker pen and let dry. Glue earring backs in place. If using clip-on fittings, position them so the earrings face the same direction on each ear. Apply 1 or 2 coats of varnish following instructions for drying times.

Variations on a Theme

Experimenting with simple, dramatic detail produces more striking designs (right).

To create a more textured effect, less care was taken when applying strips of newspaper. Less confident artists can paint designs in a single color and add decorative details with brilliant jewel stones (far right).

Simple Drop EARRINGS

There is a seemingly infinite variety of simple drop earring styles available, along with an extensive range of findings to make assembling them a simple task. You can choose hoops in different shapes that can be bought ready-formed for instant beading, or make your own from jeweler's wire shaped around a piece of dowel, a broom handle, or bead container. Ear studs, hooks, kidney wires, and a variety of screw fastenings and clip-on findings come with integral loops to make joining simple drops easy, and all are readily available from craft, bead, and jewelry specialists.

You can make drops and tops from all kinds of materials. The most traditional styles use beads that can be threaded in attractive groups onto hoops and head pins, or linked together individually with eye pins. Head and eye pins are joined directly or with jump rings to the loop on an earring finding or top of your choice. You can also make charms to use as drops from other elements like pewter, salt dough, and polymer modeling clays or create fun variations of the classic hoop style from ordinary wooden curtain rings. Make sure that the drops hang correctly when using other elements; sometimes you will need to use more than one jump ring to ensure the charm faces the right direction.

Use the main step-by-step project for inspiration on related designs. By using modeling clays in different colors, you can transform spring leaves into autumn leaves. By wrapping beads in attractive metal cages instead of string, you can create a more sophisticated look.

Take the time to practice turning perfect loops on head pins since this can affect how the drop falls.

Vary the size and shape of beads to create different visual effects.

To prevent the head pin slipping through larger beads, use a tiny rocaille as a stopper bead.

When making your own hoops, wrap the beaded wire around a tube to shape the curve—the tubes that hold small beads are ideal.

Hoops in different shapes and sizes can be bought from jewelry suppliers and all you need to do is add the beads you want.

Beaded
HOOPS

JUST A FEW BEADS, THE MOST BASIC FIND-INGS, and tools are all that's needed to create sensational dangle earrings in minutes. These designs illustrate the basic techniques involved, and once you have mastered them you will find yourself thinking up lots of your own variations. Most of these ideas work best with bought beads but you could mix them with your own papier-mâché or clay designs to add your own personal touch. Look for bead supplier catalogs that not only illustrate the fantastic variety of shapes, sizes, and colors available, but will also provide you with endless inspiration for different bead combinations. Choose beads in colors to match an outfit, an occasion, or simply your mood—crystal, jet, and diamanté instantly add a touch of glamour for evenings; brighter colors in clashing combinations look fun and funky; pearls mixed with almost anything look elegant and classy.

Getting Started

Each of these pairs of simple drop earrings use a different method to dangle beautiful beads. An ear wire is an uncomplicated way to gather a beaded hoop or to hang a head pin stacked with contrasting small and large beads. Use triangle bails to dangle crystal drops from ear clips decorated with cabochon stones.

You Will Need

FOR THE BEADED HOOPS
Jeweler's wire
Wire cutters
Pliers
Glass rocaille beads
2 jump rings
2 ear wires

FOR THE PEARL AND
BLUE GLASS BEAD DROPS
6 small pearls
2 larger beads in a contrasting color
2 head pins
Wire cutters
Pliers
2 ear wires

FOR CABOCHON AND
CRYSTAL DROPS
2 ear clips with integral loops
2 flat-backed cabochon stones
2 crystal drop beads
Epoxy glue
2 triangle bails
pliers

BEADED HOOPS

Cut a piece of wire approximately 3 inches / 7.5 cm long, turn a small loop at one end with pliers, and thread on beads from the other end.

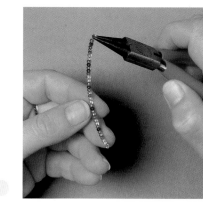

Leave enough room to turn a loop at the opposite end.

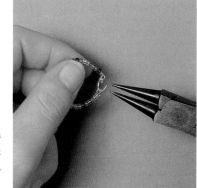

Use pliers to open up a jump ring and slip it through both loops to form a circle of beads.

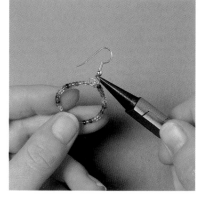

Open up the loop at the base of an ear wire with pliers. Slip the jump ring of the bead hoop into the loop and close the loop to secure.

Variations on a Theme

PEARL & BLUE GLASS DROPS

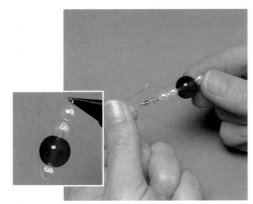

1. Thread the beads onto a head pin—the head of the pin will prevent the beads from falling off. Trim the pin with cutters, leaving enough to turn a loop using pliers.

2. Open up the loop at the base of an ear wire with pliers. Slip the loop at the top of the head pin into the loop.

3. Close up the loop to secure and complete the earrings.

CABOCHON & CRYSTAL DROPS

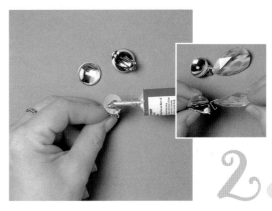

1. Glue the cabochon to the ear clip, making sure the integral loop is not obscured. Let dry completely.

2. Open up the triangle bail and slip it through the loop on the ear clip. Position the hole at the top of the crystal drop between the two sides of the triangle.

3. Close securely with pliers to complete the earrings.

Jeweled Punched Tin
DANGLES

Design Tips

Experiment with different shapes. A square is easy to begin with but the options are endless: flowers, fish, and hearts are just a few examples.

◎

Treat the metal like fabric and clip into curves to turn under edges. On intricate shapes this may be impossible, so smooth edges with a fine metal file.

◎

If your design feels flimsy and is easily bent out of shape, back it with a piece of suede, leather, or thick cardboard.

◎

Punching a design is only one idea. The metal is so soft you can also work relief designs.

◎

Pewter is not the only metal you can use. It is possible to buy copper, tin, and aluminum in sheets. You can also recycle household cans as long as they aren't too thick—traditional square olive oil cans are ideal, as are aluminum soft drink cans. (In the case of round cans, wash, dry, and lay the metal out flat under something heavy.)

WORKING WITH METAL IS A DAUNTING THOUGHT for many people since it is often assumed that special skills or expensive equipment is required. A great deal depends on the metal you choose to work with. The sheet pewter used for this project couldn't be easier to use since it is a soft metal that can be cut and shaped like fabric using heavy-duty scissors or a craft knife. This design is simple to produce, but once you gain a little experience and get used to the feel of the metal, it can be used to create very special pieces of jewelry. Pewterwork is a popular craft on its own. To find inspiration for more complicated designs, consult the many books and manuals that illustrate all the different techniques.

You Will Need

A small piece of sheet pewter
Cutting mat
Ballpoint pen
Steel ruler
Scissors
Darning needle
Small hammer
Panel pin
Piece of board
2 jewel stones
Epoxy or cement glue
Jump rings
2 eye pins or head pins
Coordinating beads
2 earring wires

Getting Started

You can use a pair of scissors to cut thin metal, but beware—the metal will blunt the cutting edge of the scissors. Try tin cutters to snip through thicker metals. For best results when cutting the metal, work on an old cutting board.

JEWELED PUNCHED TIN DANGLES

1. Place the metal sheet on top of a cutting mat and use a ballpoint pen and a steel ruler to draw a square, ¾ inch / 2 cm wide, then a border within that square ¼ inch / .5 cm wide. Press down firmly with the pen to indent the metal.

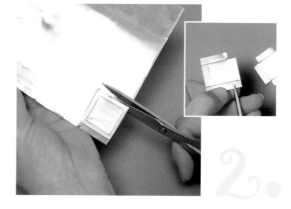

2. Cut out each shape cleanly, cutting along the border edges. Cut out tiny squares in each corner as illustrated using the tips of your scissors.

4. With the cutting mat on top of a piece of board, mark the outline of the punched design with the tip of a darning needle, making light indentations. Placing the point of the panel pin over an indentation, hammer out the design, piercing the metal.

3. Fold over the border edges along the indented lines to enclose the pen lines. Trim corners to neaten if necessary.

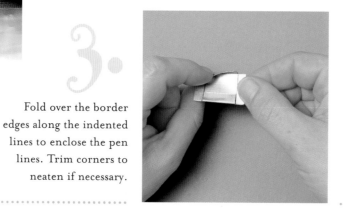

Use the hammer and panel pin to make a hole in a corner of each square. Glue jewel stones in place and let dry completely. Open up a jump ring and slip through each hole.

Snip the head end off a head pin and turn a loop using pliers. Insert the jump ring through the loop and close it securely. Add beads in the required order, trim the head pin using wire cutters, leaving enough length to turn another loop.

Open up the loop at the base of an ear wire using pliers and slip it through the loop on the head pin. Close it again to secure.

Variations on a Theme

A shell quilting pattern inspired the design for these pretty copper earrings. The motif was drawn to size on tracing paper and then the outline followed with the point of a knitting needle. Work on top of a wad of newspaper to get better relief (right).

This motif was inspired by a heraldic coat of arms (far right).

Wrapped
WITH STYLE

Design Tips

Experiment dyeing basic cotton string different colors by using natural and commercial dyes.

⊙

Create interesting effects by knotting beads onto the string, knotting the string, or tying narrow strips of fabric or thread along its length before dyeing.

⊙

When the earrings are made up, use a dry brush to stroke gold metallic paint over the string.

⊙

Sand wooden or plastic beads with an emery board to provide a good base for the glue.

⊙

Metal wire can be wrapped around glass beads for a glittering look.

⊙

Use colored cords and even cotton embroidery threads instead of plain string.

T HESE INGENIOUS EARRINGS COST NEXT-TO-
nothing to make and were inspired by a more expensive
design seen in a store. For this design, the string is
wrapped around a foam ball, but you could also use other beads
as the base if you have them in the bottom of your bead box, or
you could make your own from papier-mâché. The top of the
beads is a simple circle of thick cardboard with the string glued
to form a spiral. They look great left natural and mixed with
small wooden beads, but you could also try dyeing the string
different colors with commercial dyes or with natural
dyes like tea, onion skins, and even berries. Taking the
idea a step further, you can wrap any bead
with a coil of wire that looks just as
attractive but produces a completely
different effect.

You Will Need

Thick cardboard
Compass
Pencil
Clear-drying all-purpose craft glue
2 foam balls
A ball of cotton string
2 head pins
4 small wooden beads
6 tiny gold beads
Wire cutters
Round-nosed pliers
2 jump rings
2 earring backs
(clip-on or post fittings)

Getting Started

You will need to cut a piece of string for the cardboard disc
approximately 16 inches / 41 cm long. The length of string
needed for the foam ball will depend on the diameter of the
bead; cut a long piece to avoid having to join more string
halfway through wrapping.

WRAPPED WITH STYLE

1. Using a compass, draw 2 circles on the cardboard, each approximately ¾ inch / 2 cm in diameter, and cut out.

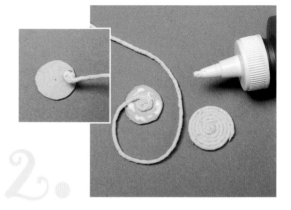

2. Roll one end of the string for the cardboard disc ¼ inch / .5 cm along its length and glue. Let dry. Cover the cardboard disc with glue and, positioning the rolled end of the string in the center, coil the string around itself to make a spiral. Taper the end of the string for a neat finish.

3. Pierce the foam ball with a toothpick and glue an end of a length of string to the edge of the top hole. Wrap the string so that it butts up to the previous round, adding dabs of glue as you work.

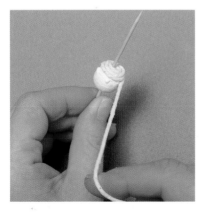

4. Glue the end neatly to the opposite end of the ball, close to the hole but not obscuring it.

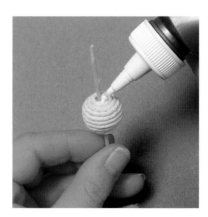

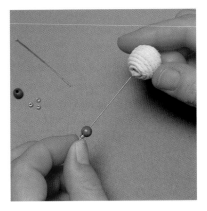

5. Thread a gold stopper bead and small wooden bead onto a head pin, insert this through the center hole of the bead and add another stopper bead, a wooden bead, and another stopper bead.

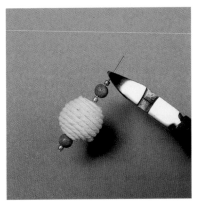

6. Trim the head with wire cutters leaving about ⅜ inch / 1 cm extending beyond the last bead. Turn a loop in remaining wire using round-nosed pliers.

7. Twist open a jump ring and ease it through the spiral earring top between the last rounds of string. Link the loop of the bead drop to the jump ring and close securely. Paint the back of the cardboard discs if required and glue earring backs in place.

Variations on a Theme

Copper wire makes a pretty cage for these frosted beads (right).
Silver wire is wrapped around crystal charms that dangle from jewel stones glued to clip-on earring backs (far right).

Gilded
FISH

Design Tips

If you don't feel confident drawing your own templates, use cookie cutters or pastry cutters to make your shapes.

◎

This project uses a simple plastic drinking straw to texture the dough to imitate fish scales. You can use all kinds of implements, from cheese graters to traditional sculpting tools, to add different textured patterns to your designs.

◎

If making your own templates, sketch out your designs on paper first. Draw them to scale to check that the earrings will be the right size and then fill in with any decorative detail you want to add.

◎

Don't forget to make a hole in the shape before it gets too hard, unless you want to glue it onto clip or post earring backs.

◎

There are a large number of different recipes for making dough—some add wallpaper paste or vegetable oil. It is a question of finding the recipe that suits you.

DOUGH SCULPTURE HAS BEEN AROUND FOR MUCH longer than people think. Ancient civilizations such as the Egyptians, Romans, and Greeks are known to have paid homage to their particular gods with figures fashioned from dough. More elaborate designs were sculpted by the Cretans to celebrate their appreciation of nature. German peasants, who used dough to make Christmas tree ornaments, added salt to the dough to protect it from being eaten by animals, especially mice. This was the real beginning of the salt dough craft as it is known today. It is a wonderfully versatile and inexpensive modeling medium. The trick is getting the dough to the right consistency, but once it is made, it can be sculpted, molded, or rolled out like pastry to create an enormous variety of designs. Painted and varnished, the dough shapes make bright, fun pieces of jewelry that cost next to nothing.

Getting Started

As you mix the ingredients for the dough, if it turns out to be too sticky, add a bit more flour; if it is too dry, add a little more water. This traditional recipe for salt dough will make far more dough than you need for this design. Wrap the extra dough in plastic in an airtight container to make it last for several days.

You Will Need

FOR DOUGH
2 cups of plain flour
1 cup of table salt
3/4 cup hot water

TO MAKE EARRINGS
Tracing paper
Pencil
Cardboard
Scissors
Mixing bowl
Fork
Rolling pin
Craft knife
Plastic drinking straw
Toothpick
Paintbrush
Gold metallic paint
Varnish
2 jump rings
2 ear hooks

GILDED FISH

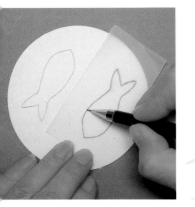

Draw a fish shape on tracing paper and transfer to cardboard. You may find it easier to draw 2 templates (a template for each earring), but it isn't essential.

Cut the template out carefully following the outline of the shape.

Place the flour in a mixing bowl and stir in the salt. Add the water slowly.

Mix all the ingredients together, first with a fork and then with your hands, until the "dough" is stiff but not too sticky. Turn it out onto a board and knead for 10 minutes, until smooth. Place the dough in a plastic bag or container for about an hour.

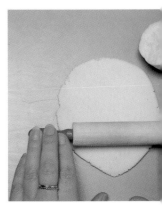

Cut off a portion of the dough and roll out to a thickness of approximately ¼ inch / .5 cm.

6.

Place the template on top of the dough and cut out the shape using a craft knife. Moisten the edges with water and smooth them out.

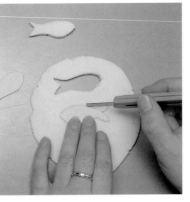

7.

Use the base of a wooden skewer to make an indentation for the eye, then make the effect of scales with a drinking straw. Use a toothpick to pierce a hole at the head end of the fish to attach the ear hook. Set the oven to 200° F / 93° C and place the design on a baking sheet. Bake until completely dry (5 to 8 hours depending on the size and thickness of the dough).

8.

Gently stroke a dry brush loaded with a little paint over the design to highlight the relief. When dry, add 1 or 2 coats of varnish. Let dry. Twist open a jump ring and insert through the hole. Link through the loop of an earring wire. Close with pliers.

Variations on a Theme

These simple but effective dough earrings were cut using a cookie cutter and then painted a vibrant pink. To link together 2 or 3 flowers, pierce holes at the top and bottom (right).

In keeping with the sea theme, these pretty starfish look as though they have been silver-plated. Pierce a hole in the top point of the star to turn into basic drops (far right).

Simple Drop Earrings **59**

Hoop
DREAMS

Design Tips

Place the curtain ring on a sheet of paper and draw around its outlines to make a template to work out more complicated designs.

⟲

You can apply the letters at random, as in this project, but place them in approximately the same position on each earring. To keep an overall balanced effect, avoid grouping too many of the same letters close together.

⟲

If you don't have the patience to complete the letter design, you can dress up curtain rings by wrapping them with colorful embroidery threads, strings of beads, or even fancy knitting yarns to give a textured finish.

⟲

Experiment with different paint effects such as marbling, sponging, and stippling to create another look.

BASIC WOODEN CURTAIN RINGS JUST CRY OUT TO BE turned into fabulous hoop earrings. They provide the perfect base for all kinds of clever decorative effects and come complete with a ready-made loop that is easy to join to an ear hook. They can be wrapped with an endless variety of materials from braids to beads, and painted with imaginative designs or ornate marbled, sponged, or stippled finishes. The inspiration for this project came after an evening of filing, the mind wandering, and wondering what other surfaces rub-on letters could be applied to. The result are these fun earrings, which are destined to be a conversation starter. The design opportunities are endless—you can rub on the letters to form words, sentences, sayings, and even incorporate your name. It is a little time-consuming and a challenge rubbing the letters onto a curved surface but the finished result is worth the effort.

You Will Need

FOR ABC EARRINGS
2 wooden curtain rings
Artist's gesso
White cold ceramic paint
Black rub-on letters
A wooden skewer
Varnish
2 earring hooks
Round-nosed pliers

〜

FOR RAINBOW HOOPS
2 wooden curtain rings
Embroidery thread
Craft glue
2 earring hooks
Round-nosed pliers

Getting Started

Practice rubbing the letters onto paper first so that you can get the feel of them—some are more fragile than others and need a bit of extra care when applying them. It helps to cut out the letters in small, manageable strips.

HOOP DREAMS

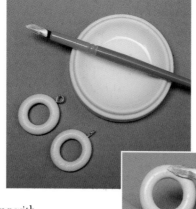

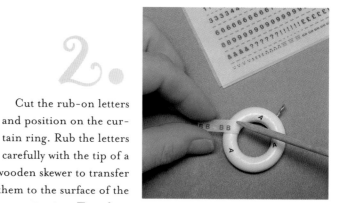

1. Paint each ring with an undercoat of artist's gesso. Let dry. Paint the rings with white ceramic paint and let dry.

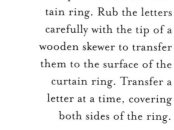

2. Cut the rub-on letters and position on the curtain ring. Rub the letters carefully with the tip of a wooden skewer to transfer them to the surface of the curtain ring. Transfer a letter at a time, covering both sides of the ring.

4. Using pliers, twist open the loop at the bottom of an ear wire, push it through the brass loop on the curtain ring, and close again to secure.

3. Paint both rings with 1 or 2 coats of varnish.

Variations on a Theme

RAINBOW HOOPS

1. Select 6 or 7 colors of embroidery thread and cut each into lengths of 18 inches / 46 cm. Use curtain rings that have been painted with an undercoat of gesso and then with ceramic paint, as in steps 1 and 2 of *Hoop Dreams*.

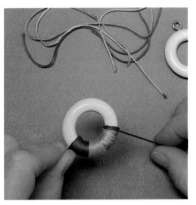

2. Glue the end of a length of embroidery to the curtain ring and let it dry. When secure, wrap the rest of the length tightly around the ring, covering it completely. Glue the next color in the same way and wrap over the end of the previous color to disguise the joint.

3. Wrap and join the remaining colors as before.

Wrap strings of small beads around a wooden curtain ring, like the embroidery threads. Try wrapping the beads loosely to show background colors, as shown here (right).

Ivy LEAVES

TODAY'S SYNTHETIC MODELING CLAYS ARE A WONDER-fully versatile modeling medium for craft jewelry designers to work with. They are soft and malleable, and once the clay has been kneaded and warmed in your hands, it is simple to sculpt, mold, or cut into a variety of shapes. The range of available colors is extensive and can be used on their own or blended together to create spectacular marbled effects. Rolled out like pastry, the clay is ideal for using with cookie cutters, cardboard templates, and found objects like the leaves that inspired these pretty earrings. The clay is so soft it is possible to imprint the shape of a leaf and its veins, which is then cut out with a craft knife. Two of the greatest advantages these polymer clays have over traditional cold clays is that they set hard quickly in a low-temperature domestic oven and won't shatter if dropped. A coat of varnish increases the depth of the colors and produces a finish similar to kiln-fired ceramics.

Getting Started

Knead the Fimo with your thumbs and fingers until very soft and pliable. This will make it much easier to roll and will prevent cracks. Wash your hands when changing colors to prevent one rubbing off on the other and spoiling the finished effect.

You Will Need

2 blocks of Fimo,
1 white and 1 green
Rolling pin
1 or 2 fallen ivy leaves
Craft knife
Thick needle
2 jump rings
2 ear hooks
Varnish
Paintbrush
Pliers

IVY LEAVES

Break off a piece of Fimo from each block, knead, and roll out into log shapes. Wrap the 2 colors around each other and roll again to form a single log shape. Fold this in half, twist the 2 halves together and knead to blend the colors together. Continue twisting and kneading until you get a marbled effect.

Roll the clay out like pastry on a flat surface to a thickness of approximately ¼ inch / .5 cm.

Place leaves on top of Fimo with the vein side directly on the clay.

To get a deeper impression use a rolling pin to press the leaves into the clay. Very carefully cut out around the outline of each leaf using a craft knife. Give the edges of each leaf as much detail as possible.

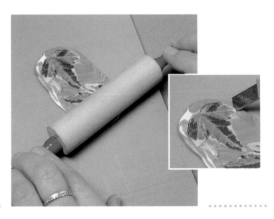

5.

Use a needle to pierce a hole at the stalk end of each leaf to attach the ear fitting, then fire in a low-temperature oven as recommended on the packet instructions.

6.

Twist open the jump rings and insert through the pierced holes and the loop at the bottom of any ear hook. Close the jump rings securely using pliers.

7.

Paint each leaf with a few coats of varnish to give depth to the marbled colors.

Variations on a Theme

For a striking autumnal feel, select different leaf shapes and change the colors used to marble the clay to red and brown (right).

More stylized leaf shapes can be cut from plain Fimo using a cardboard template and craft knife (far right).

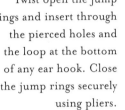

Multidrop & Linked
EARRINGS

The same basic techniques described to make simple drop earrings can be extended to make more extravagant drop and link designs. Use more than one drop, vary the lengths of the strand, join and link several of the same elements together, and vary the color combinations. Look for decorative spacers, ear and necklace hangers, necklace ends, bead cups, bell caps, and even clasps to create wonderfully original earrings. Try adding buttons, sequins, and even children's tiddly-winks to enrich your designs. Sequins come in all shapes and sizes and have the advantage of being as light as a feather. You can also make your own earrings from polymer clays, air-dry clays, and papier-mâché shapes. What you choose to use depends on the style of the earrings, whether they are clip-on, post and butterfly, or hook fittings.

As you develop your multidrop designs, it is important to create a balanced, completed design that won't overpower the shape of your face or get lost in your hairstyle. If you use more than one strand, make sure the earrings hang correctly. The design should be perfectly balanced so it doesn't tilt to one side. You may need to use more than one jump ring to ensure the drop or charm faces the right direction. These are things that come with practice and are possible to correct if you don't get it right the first time.

Feel free to experiment with techniques and materials to create variations on the projects shown here. For example, by swapping paper for textured paint, papier-mâché earring bases are completely transformed. Try using different cutters or paint effects on air-dry clay to increase the design options tenfold.

Sketch out design ideas on paper to experiment with different color combinations and sizes and shapes of beads.

It is important to get the strands to balance correctly or the earrings will look lopsided.

Vary the number and length of the bead strands to create different effects.

One single strand of large beads can look quite dramatic hung from the center hole.

Experiment with different styles and shapes of bell caps. Fluted bell caps conceal the connection between the top of the beaded strands, making it look like a beaded tassel.

Shades of Blue
EARRINGS

THE FILIGREE BELL CAPS USED TO MAKE THESE earrings are just one of the many decorative findings available and are multipurpose, too. Here they are used to dangle bead strands, but they can also be used on both sides of a bead to make it look more special or to begin and end a necklace or bracelet. The ready-made holes around the edges are perfect for joining bead strands using a jump ring. The central hole can be wired with a longer strand and provide the link for an ear wire. This style of earring can be bold and striking or pretty and delicate, depending on the size of the bell cap and the beads used for the dangles.

You Will Need

2 filigree bell caps
Beads
Eye pins
Wire cutters
Pliers
2 ear wires
Jump rings

Getting Started

Select beads in several shades of the same color and in a few varied sizes. Remember that you don't have to thread bead strands through all of the holes on the filigree bell caps; this project uses only 4 strands per earring.

SHADES OF BLUE EARRINGS

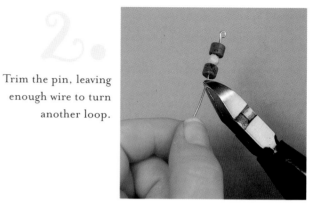

2. Trim the pin, leaving enough wire to turn another loop.

1. Thread the beads in groups or singularly onto an eye pin.

3. To make the strands, open up a jump ring and slip through the loops of 2 beaded pins. Close the ring securely. Join as many beaded pins together as necessary to get the length required.

5. Before closing the ring, slip it through the loop at the end of a bead strand, then close securely.

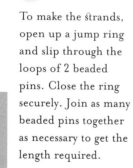

4. Open up the jump rings and slip through the holes around the end of the bell cap.

6. Add as many strands as you wish to the edge of the bell cap, then insert an eye pin through the central hole so that the preformed loop sits on top of the cap. Trim the pin and turn a loop at the other end.

7. Join the central strand to the last loop with a jump ring. Close securely.

8. To complete the earrings, open up the loop at the bottom of an ear wire and slip through the central loop on the top of the bell cap. Close securely.

Variations on a Theme

These triangles have predrilled holes along the bottom edge and top point of the triangle. Beads have been wired onto head pins and linked to the finding with jump rings (right).

The striking copper hanger that forms the base for these earrings was taken from a broken necklace. Rocaille beads have been threaded onto head pins and linked to the hanger with jump rings (far right).

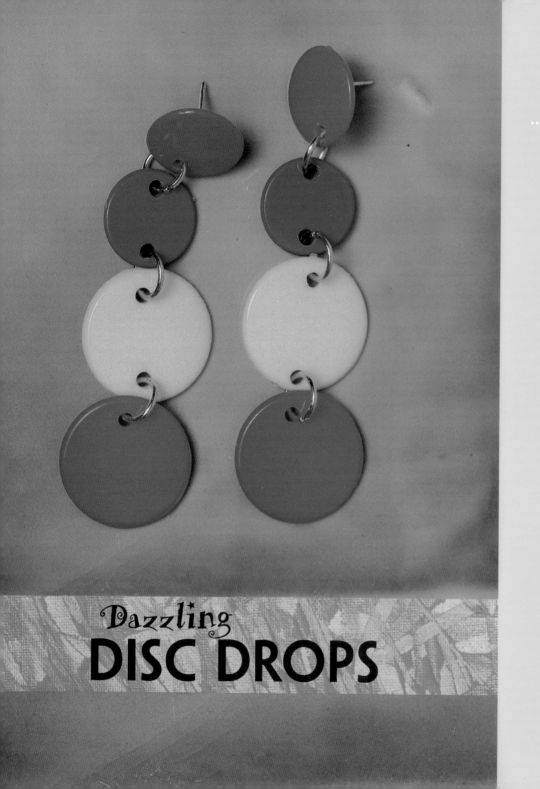

Give tiddlywinks a more glamorous look by decorating them with flat-backed jewel stones or hand-painted designs.

Use sequin shapes like flowers, hearts, stars, and moons to create pretty drops.

Measure and mark the position of holes to ensure the earrings hang correctly.

Mix the discs or sequins with coordinating or contrasting beads for a different look.

Children's games can be a great source of inspiration for fun designs. If you can use a drill, you can link together different three-dimensional shapes, such as playing pieces from a game.

Dazzling
DISC DROPS

I F YOU SET ASIDE TRADITIONAL INFLUENCES and use a little lateral thinking, you can transform the most unlikely materials into witty, wearable pieces of jewelry. The brilliantly colored discs from a child's game of tiddlywinks and shimmering large sequins are used to create these fun drop earrings and are just a few examples of what you can do. Holes are easy to make in plastic using a sharp bradawl or a hand drill with a fine bit. You can link as many tiddlywinks together as you like, using different colors and sizes like the design shown here. The same basic principles can be applied to a dazzling collection of sequins, which can be easily pierced with a sharp needle.

You Will Need

FOR PRIMARY DROPS
Tiddlywinks
Ruler
China marking pencils or
felt-tip marker pen
Plasticine
Hand drill with fine bit
6 jump rings
Earring backs (clip-on or post fittings)
All-purpose clear-drying glue
Pliers

✧

FOR SHIMMERING SEQUINS
Round and oval sequins
Sharp needle
Piece of cork
10 jump rings
2 ear hooks
Pliers

Getting Started

Lay the tiddlywinks on a flat surface in the order they are to be linked together. The top and bottom discs only require one hole but the middle discs will need two. Use a ruler to align the marks for the holes in the discs.

DAZZLING DISC DROPS

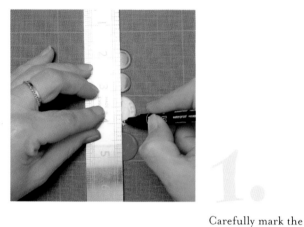

Working on a piece of plywood or old cutting board, press the tiddly-wink into a lump of plasticine to hold it firmly in place and drill the holes as marked.

Carefully mark the position of the holes close to the edge.

Twist open a jump ring and push it through the hole on the first disc and the top hole on the next disc. Close securely with pliers. Link the rest together in the same way.

Glue an earring back to the reverse side of the top disc to complete the earring. Dazzling sequins can be linked together using the same basic principles.

Variations on a Theme

SHIMMERING SEQUINS

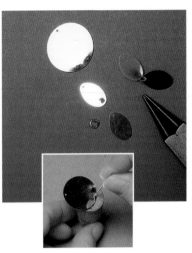

Place the sequins on top of a piece of cork and pierce the marked holes with a sharp needle. Twist open the jump rings and insert through the pierced holes to link the sequins together.

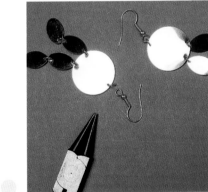

Use a sharp needle to mark the position of a hole close to the edge on a large disc sequin and 2 holes close to the opposite edge in line with 2 oval sequins as shown. Place another 2 oval sequins below the first pair and mark the position for holes in the bottom of the first and the top of the second pairs.

Insert a jump ring through the top hole and the loop at the bottom of an ear hook.

Close securely with pliers. Sequins are extremely fine and will slip through any gap in the jump ring.

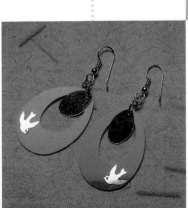

Decorate a large, open, oval sequin with a tiny sequin bird, using a dab of glue to hold it in place. Choose another sequin shape to hang in the center of the oval, pierce corresponding holes, and link together with jump rings (right).

Jewel Bright
TRIANGLES

Design Tips

Start a collection of foil candy wrappers to use for lots of different designs. Smooth them out, and keep them flat and protected in a cardboard box.

✺

Sketch out your design on paper and work out a color scheme before cutting out your cardboard base shape.

✺

Once you have mastered the papier-mâché technique, you can experiment using all kinds of different paper in the final layer—not just decorative foil, but also handmade papers and even wrapping paper.

✺

Protect design and papers with one or two coats of varnish.

✺

Experiment with different shapes. Start with simple geometric shapes and gradually work your way up to more complicated, creative designs.

✺

Read the directions for making perfect papier-mâché in the design tips for *Colorful Contemporary Earrings*.

These glitzy earrings were inspired by the brightly colored foil paper used to wrap chocolate candy. The colored wrappers, which are almost as edible as the candy, are used as the final layer on a papier-mâché base shape. Layering is one of the easiest papier-mâché techniques and is where pasted strips of torn paper are smoothed in layers over a base shape or mold. The technique is very simple to master and needs just a bit of care when building up the layers to ensure they are smooth, without air bubbles or lumps of paste (unless you want a textured finish). The geometric shape of the earrings is ideal for this kind of bold decoration but they would look equally stylish with handmade paper used as a final layer or even textured, glitter paints.

You Will Need

Cardboard
Pencil
Ruler
Scissors
Wallpaper paste
Paste brush
Artist's gesso
Thick needle
Brightly colored foil candy wrappers
All-purpose craft glue
12 small gold beads
12 head pins
Wire cutters
Pliers
18 jump rings
Earring backs (clip-on or post fittings)

Getting Started

You only need to make up a small amount of wallpaper paste for these earrings. Tear up enough small newspaper strips so that each earring shape has 4 to 6 layers in all for a firm, finished piece.

JEWEL BRIGHT TRIANGLES

1. On cardboard, draw out 2 squares, ½ inch / 1 cm long and 2 triangles, whose sides are 1½ inch / 4 cm long.

2. Carefully cut out shapes, making sure edges are smooth. Paste a strip of newspaper and place on one side of the shape so that a little extends beyond the edge. Smooth flat with your fingers.

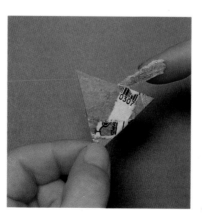

3. Smooth the protruding end over to the opposite side, making sure it is wrinkle-free on the edge. Continue layering over all 4 shapes, covering both sides and all edges. For a durable finish, paint the last couple with PVA glue instead of paste.

4. Paint the earrings with artist's gesso. This acts as an undercoat and prevents the newsprint from showing through the painted finish.

Using a ruler as a guide, mark the position of 6 holes along one edge of the triangle.

6.

Pierce the marked holes using a sharp, thick needle. Pierce additional holes in the top point of the triangle and in a corner of the small square.

7.

Cover triangles and squares with foil paper, and glue in place. Pierce all holes again through the foil. Cut out a triangle in a contrasting color foil, and glue it in the center of the triangle. Glue a small flat-backed jewel stone in the center of this. Insert jump rings through holes at the top of the triangle and corner of the square. Close and use a third jump ring to link the 2 pieces together. Slip tiny gold beads onto head pins, trim to ⅜ inch / 1 cm, and turn a loop. Insert jump rings through the holes along the bottom of the triangle and the loop of the bead charm. Close securely. Glue earring backs in place.

Variations on a Theme

Vary the basic shapes and combine pretty handmade paper with coppery foil for a different effect (right).

Use textured glitter paints to jazz up the basic papier-mâché shapes and add a touch of sparkle (far right).

Make a sketch of your design idea before starting, work out the colors and sizes, and then count to make sure you have enough buttons.

◎

Use larger buttons for the legs to give the impression of trousers and work the body and arms in the same color to look like a sweater.

◎

Use strong cotton or invisible thread to work the design.

◎

Make sure both legs and both arms are strung with the identical buttons, in the same order.

◎

Try making your own buttons with polymer clays or air-dry clays.

Button People
EARRINGS

U SING BUTTONS AS FASTENINGS ON CLOTHES IS NOT the only way to admire their beauty, color, and shape. They can also be linked and strung together like beads to make innovative jewelry designs. Lots of people have wonderful collections of buttons that never see the light of day and these whimsical earrings are the perfect way to show them off. It is simply the way they are strung together that creates the effect of arms, legs, and bodies. Once you have mastered the basic button technique, you can have fun giving the button people individual characteristics and use buttons in different colors to give them the appearance of wearing trousers and a top. Glue larger buttons at different angles to give the idea of a jaunty hat. Keep both sides of the design the same and choose buttons of similar sizes to create a balanced look overall.

20 to 28 buttons for 4 arms
20 to 28 buttons for 4 legs
6 to 10 larger buttons for bodies
2 to 4 buttons for necks
2 buttons for hats
8 small beads for hands and feet
2 larger beads for heads
Strong cotton or invisible thread
Needle
2 ear hooks
All-purpose clear-drying glue

Getting Started

Cut 2 lengths of thread, each approximately 18 inches / 46 cm long. The small beads, which will look like hands and feet, will act like stopper beads for the buttons on the arms and legs.

BUTTON PEOPLE EARRINGS

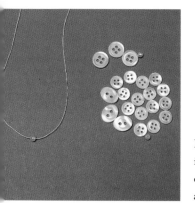

Fold a length of thread in half and insert one end through the hole in a small bead.

To make a leg, take one end of the length of thread through a hole in a button and take the other end through a hole directly opposite the first. Repeat. Make the other leg in the same way.

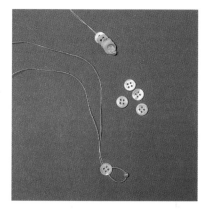

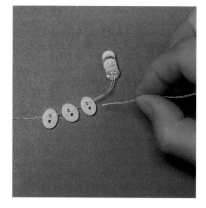

Take both ends of thread from a leg and insert through the same hole on a larger button for the body. Add 2 or 3 buttons as required. Insert both ends of thread from the second leg through an opposite hole.

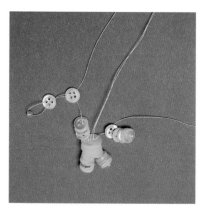

To make an arm, separate the pair of threads on one side and take only one through a hole in each button. When the arm is long enough, push the thread through a small bead and then back up the arm through the holes directly opposite the first. Work the other arm in the same way.

5. Add 1 or 2 buttons to make the neck, threading buttons onto the thread as for the body. Insert all ends of thread through a bead to make the "head."

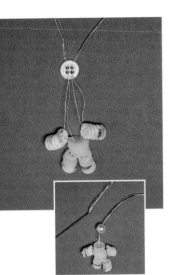

6. Add a button to make a hat, taking the threads through a hole and back through the opposite. Secure the thread with a knot and a dab of glue.

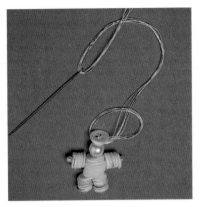

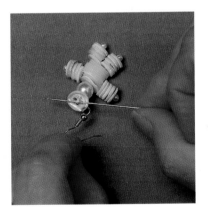

7. Twist open the loop at the bottom of an earring hook and push it under the threads on the hat. Close to secure.

Variations on a Theme

Horn and mother-of-pearl buttons are combined with wooden beads in this alternative (right).

A collection of pretty pastel buttons has been mixed with transparent buttons and blue beads to create this effect (far right).

As you sketch out your design ideas and work out the scale and balance of the idea, remember that the earrings shouldn't be too large. They should also be linked together so they hang properly.

Mix a little air-dry clay with water to make a paste that you can brush over the surface to fill in any cracks.

Smooth rough edges with an emery board.

Experiment with different paint effects and a variety of shaped cutters. Visit a professional kitchen supply shop to find molds and cutters in all kinds of designs.

Hearts of
GOLD

T

HESE PRETTY HEART earrings were inspired by a Coco Chanel design that appeared in *Vogue* magazine. The new design is interpreted in a slightly different way and doesn't contain all the elements of the original, but the earrings still look stylish and chic. They are easy to make from a modern air-dry clay that gives a wonderful ceramic finish without the need for an expensive kiln. Painted with special cold ceramic paints, air-dry clay really does mimic china and porcelain. It is easy to mold, sculpt, and cut just like polymer clays and can be substituted for all the projects that don't rely on the poly clay colors (you won't get the same marbled or millefiori effects even with clever paint techniques).

Getting Started

After you cut out the heart shapes from the clay, smooth their edges with a damp paintbrush or your fingers. Wait to trim the eye pins that are insert-ed into the hearts until after you paint the piece—the length of the pins makes the hearts easier to paint.

You Will Need

Air-dry clay
Rolling pin
Heart-shaped cutters in small and medium sizes
8 eye pins
Wire cutters
Superglue
Artist's gesso
Paintbrush
Red acrylic enamel paint
Gold Plaka paint
Chain
10 jump rings
Pliers
2 earring backs
(clip-on or post fittings)

HEARTS OF GOLD

1. Roll out the clay on a flat surface to a thickness of approximately ¼ inch / .5 cm.

2. Cut out 2 medium hearts and 6 small hearts.

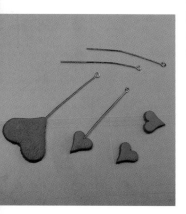

3. Insert an eye pin ¼ inch / .5 cm into the clay at the bottom of the 2 larger hearts and at the top of the 6 small hearts. Leave them until they set hard, with no signs of moisture.

4. Paint each heart with gesso. When dry, gently ease the eye pins out from the clay, trim so that only the eye extends beyond the clay and insert them back in the holes. Use a dab of superglue to secure them in place.

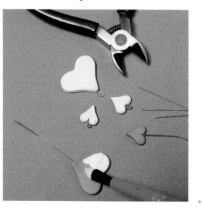

5. Paint both sides of the small hearts gold and the larger hearts red. Let dry.

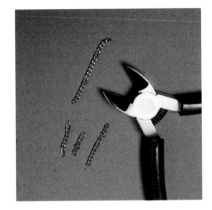

6. Divide the chain into 3 different lengths for each earring, snipping the links with wire cutters.

7. Slip the top link of each chain onto a jump ring. Attach a small heart to the bottom of each chain with a jump ring slipped through the last chain link and the eye on the heart. Join the heart drops to the earring top with a jump ring inserted through the eye on the main heart and the jump ring at the top of the drop.

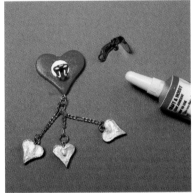

8. Glue an earring back to the reverse side of the top heart.

Variations on a Theme

Stars and moons are a celestial combination that always works well. The clay motifs shown here have been painted silver and linked together with a crystal bead (right).

Air-dry clay provides a wonderful base for paint techniques as these oak leaf and acorn earrings illustrate (far right).

Acknowledgments

Grateful thanks to the many people without whose help and support this book would not have been published. First and most important, to my parents for their endless patience and for turning a blind eye when I used their home as a design studio. To Lindsey Stock and Jackie Schou for their additional design ideas, and to Paul Forrester for his creative photography. And, finally, to Shawna Mullen and Martha Wetherill, who made sense of everything I have written and gave valuable support and encouragement when times got tough.

About the Author

Jo Moody is a journalist who specializes in fashion and craft, and who has spent many years working for women's magazines. She is now a freelance stylist and writer, contributing features and designs to a variety of publications. Her childhood fascination with jewelry has developed into a passion—she loves rediscovering traditional crafts and using them in new ways to transform everyday things into truly beautiful jewelry.

index

A

acrylic paints, 14
adhesives, 7
air-dry clay, 86–89

B

beads
    calculating, 19
    clay, 14–15
    fabric, 16
    glass, 35–37
    ideas for, 14–17
    making, 14–17
    millefiori, 15
    paper, 16
    papier-mâché, 16
    piercing, 14
    pressed cotton, 17
    round, 15
    square, 15
    tube, 14
    wooden, 17
bell caps, 6, 10, 12, 13, 70–73
buttons, 30, 82–85
button-style earrings, 30–33

C

calotte crimps, 6, 7, 12, 13
canvas, 29
cardboard, 39–40, 53–55, 58
clay, 14–15
    beads, 14–15
    for millefiori, 15
    marbling, 15
    polymer, 14–15, 64–67
    safety precautions for, 15
cookie cutters, 56, 65, 87, 88
copper, 51, 73
copper wire, 55

D

cork, 22–25
creating a design, 18–19
crimp beads, 13
curtain rings, 60–63

decorative clasps, 11
design techniques, 18–19
drop earrings, 42–67
    making, 9–10

E

ear clips, 5
ear hooks, 5
ear wire, 45
earring fittings, 5
embroidering, 26–29
eye pins, 6, 7, 8, 9, 10, 11, 12, 13, 43

F

fabric, 14, 30–33
    beads, 16
    painting, 30–33
feathers, 14
felt, 26–29
findings, 5–6, 10–13
finishing techniques, 12–13
foil, 14, 17, 78–79, 81

G

glass beads, 35–37
glue, 7
gutta resist, 31–32

H

hangers, 6, 10–11
head pins, 6, 7, 8, 11, 43, 45
hoop earrings, 43, 44–46, 60–63
hoops, 5

J

jeweler's wire, 6, 7, 9
jump rings, 5, 7, 8, 9, 10, 11, 12, 71

K

kidney wires, 43

L

linked earrings, 68–89
linking beads, 8–9
linking findings, 7, 12–13
linking multidrop earrings, 10–11

M

making spirals, 25
marbling, 15, 64–67
metal, 48
metal spacers, 13
metal washers, 17
millefiori, 15
multidrop earrings, 10–11, 68–89

N

needle-nosed pliers, 7, 13
nylon line, 13

P

painting earrings, 41, 59, 88
papier-mâché, 16, 38–41, 78–81
pearls, 37
pewter, 48–51
plasticine, 16–17
pliers
    needle-nosed, 7, 13
    round-nosed, 7, 8, 13
polymer clay, 14, 64–67
position, 21
posts, 5
pressed cotton beads, 17

R

round-nosed pliers, 7, 8, 13
    for turning loops, 7

S

safety precautions for polymer clay, 15
salt dough, 17, 56–59
sequins, 74–77
silver wire, 55
size, 21
spacers, 6
stopper beads, 8
string, 52–55
stud earrings, 20–41

T

tassels, 36–37, 72–73, 81
tiddlywinks, 74–77
tiger tail, 13
tin, 48–51
tools, 7
triangle bails, 45, 47
turning loops, 7

W

wire cutters, 7, 8, 13
wooden beads, 17
working out a design, 19

Sketch your ideas...